Dirt & Other Works

cover:
Dirt
studio floor dirt swept onto glued cardboard, 1972

Dirt & Other Works

Les Coleman

Coracle 2009

With support from The Elephant Trust

Coracle
Ballybeg, Grange, Clonmel, Tipperary, Ireland
ISBN 978–0–906630–39–6
Copyright © Les Coleman, David Briers, 2009
Designed by Colin Sackett
Printed and bound in China

Distributed by Cornerhouse Publications
70 Oxford Street, Manchester M1 5NH
www.cornerhouse.org

Pollock's Palette

Household paint on hardboard, 1972

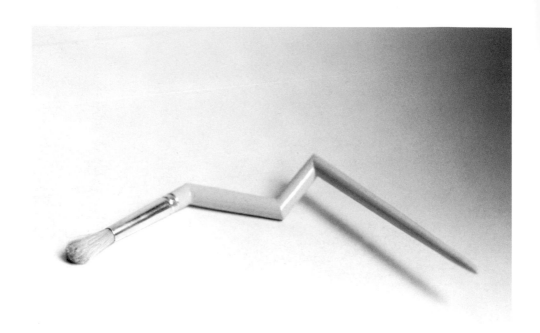

Cubist Paintbrush

Adapted brush, 1970

Revenge

Hammer, nail, 1971

Game for One

Adapted table-tennis bat with ball, 1971

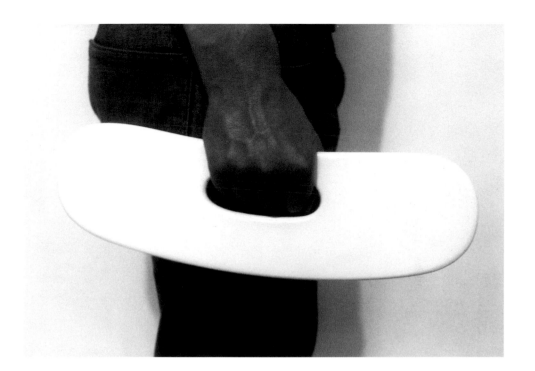

Negative / Positive

Cellulose on plywood, 1971

Dust Trap

Cartridge paper, household paint, 1973

Pencil and Rubber

Pencil shavings, rubber, 1973

Three Jam Jars

Jam jars, 1975

1lb of Sugar

Sugar cubes, 1975

Stencil

Sawdust, 1973

A book is placed on a table so that it overlaps the edge. The overlapping section is then cut off along the line of the table edge and positioned directly below on the floor.

Gravity
1975

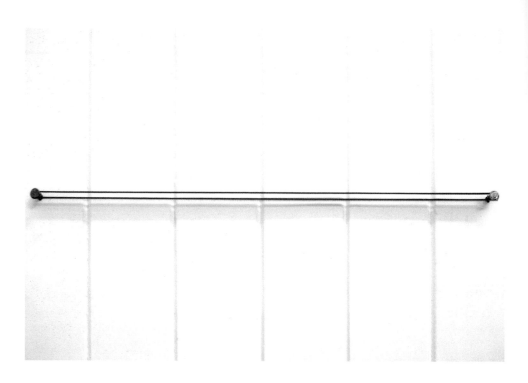

Tension

Rubber band, nails, 1975

Air and Water

Glasses, water, table-tennis balls, 1975

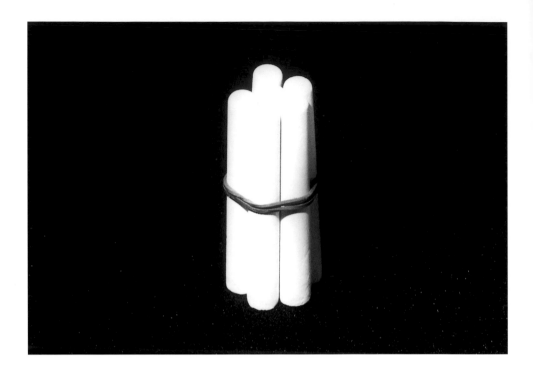

Chalks

Blackboard chalks, rubber band, 1975

Watercolour

Shelf, jam jars, dyed water, 1976

Target

Lard, tiddlywinks, 1977

Stillborn

Galvanised bucket, water, balloons, 1977

Oil and Water and Two Dead Flies

Glass, oil, water, flies, 1977

Choose a red and a white wine to be drunk at an exhibition opening. The show consists of two photographs, one of a glass of red wine, one of a glass of the white wine. Framed and presented on opposing walls they are titled by name, country of origin and year of bottling. Decide on a date and time to hold the private view and send out invitations. The exhibition lasts just for the opening.

Private View
Unrealised proposal, Coracle Press, London, 1978

Drips

Curtain wire, eyelets, hooks, glycerine, 1978

Sugar, Glucose Syrup, Citric Acid, Sodium Pyrophosphate,
Acid Calcium Phosphate, Stabiliser, Flavouring, Ascorbic Acid,
Calcium Carbonate, Sodium Nitrate, Saccharin, Colour.

Ice lolly, 1978

A galvanized wheelbarrow filled
to its rim with mercury.

Pond
1979

MINE   YOURS   OURS   THEIRS

Possession

Apples, engraved labels, 1980

England v. Italy

Electric fire and fan wired into a single electric plug, 1981

12 Fournier Street, London E1

Saloon car, adhesive letters, 1981

TCP

Glass saucers, liquid antiseptic, 1981

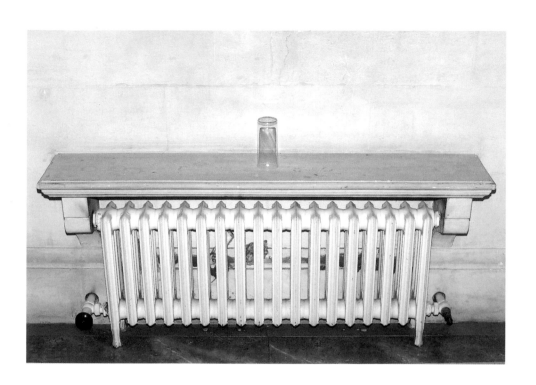

Milk Tooth

Glass, tooth, 1981

A photographic slide of a thermometer projected life-size directly on to the real thermometer.

Projected Temperature
1982

Live and Dead Batteries

Batteries, 1982

A simple four-foot wide bed is positioned centrally within an empty room. A mattress is placed on top and covered with a sheet tucked in. Further mattresses and sheets are stacked until the ceiling is reached.

Column
1982

Crossfire

Adapted archery arrows, 1982/2007

Dividing Line

Cut postcard reproductions of 20th century art, 1983

Some Aspects of Contemporary Art Seen as a Disassembled Tool

Publications of artists' work from the 1970s, Stanley block plane components, 1983

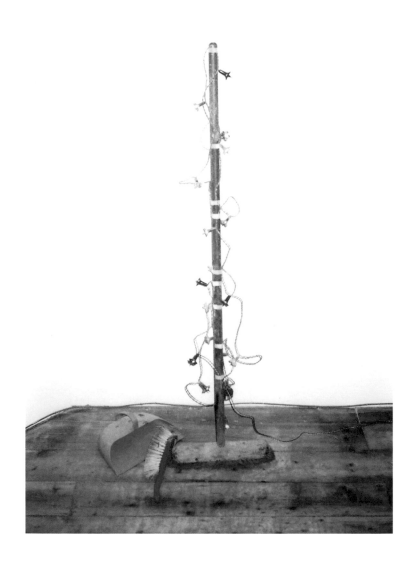

25th December

Broom, dustpan and brush, fairy lights, 1982

The Little Green Aeroplane Joins In

Television, plastic toy, 1983

360°

Adapted atlas, 1984

Survival Circle

Floor with textured paint, metal puzzles, live snails, lettuce leaf, 1984

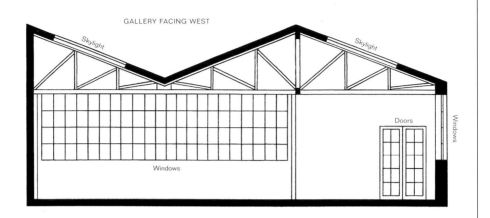

Rocks are thrown from outside the gallery space until every window has been broken. The residue of this action is left to act as the exhibit. Use grant allocation to reglaze on closure of the exhibition.

Debris

Unrealised proposal, Matt's Gallery, London, 1984

Anyone for Sculpture?

Found tennis ball, plinth with perspex box, tennis racket, rope barrier, 1988

Odd Balls

Engraved plaque: Anyone who paints a sky green and grass blue should be
sterilised.—Adolf Hitler, shopping trolley, shrink-wrapped framed prints, 1988

A number of galvanized buckets are lined up around the walls of a gallery. At the beginning of the exhibition these are full of water. A gas cylinder stands with a rubber hose attached to a small, centrally placed, gas ring. A stainless steel container is placed on the gas ring and for the duration of the exhibition water is boiled away from the buckets.

Steam
1988

Good Boy

Window display including canvas, easel, dog bowl and lead, dummy surveillance camera, 1990

Regatta

Four-drawer filing cabinet, folded computer paper boats, water, three drawers
labelled 'Nothing', 1991

Accident

China ornament, plinth, engraved label, 1991

Haven

Goldfish bowl, oil, ball bearings, 1991

The next day's date is displayed on a billboard each day for one year. Commencing on the 31st December the date is changed each day at midnight.

A Year in Advance
Unrealised proposal, Billboard Project, Birmingham, 1992

Hammersmith Broadway

Slide projections, looped tape recording, 1993

Mind Over Matter

Stack of books, concealed bracket, 1994

National Pride

Flag, 1994

A PILE OF KNIVES AND FORKS WHOSE

SUMMIT IS 29,028 FEET ABOVE SEA LEVEL

Unrealisable Sculpture
1995

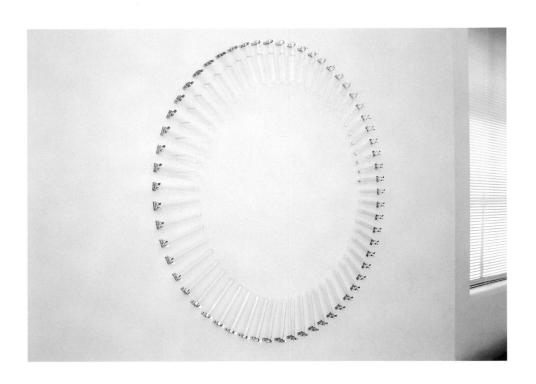

The Effect of Gravity on Water

Test-tubes, tool clips, water, 1995

Table and Chair

Adapted table, chair, 1995

Entrance

Adapted door and frame, 1995

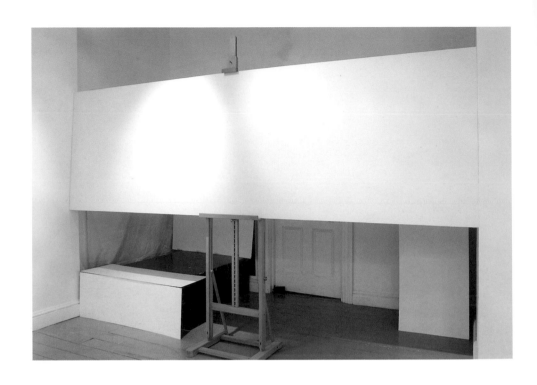

Wall to Wall
Canvas, easel, 1995

Work and Play

Adapted pack of cards, card table, plumb-line, cleat, 1995

A table tennis table with fitted net is placed centrally in an empty room. A circle cut from the centre of each half of the table allows loudspeakers to be fitted. A tape loop of a table tennis game is played through the speakers.

Ping-Pong
1996

Place Setting

Adapted table, chair, plates, knife and fork, 1996

Losing Weight

Candle, scales, 1996

A four-drawer office filing cabinet is heated from the inside by concealed gas jets directed onto the cabinet walls. The metal glows a fierce red, throwing out an intense heat. There is nothing to stop the cabinet being approached.

Danger
1999

A–Z of Dog-ears

Adapted book, 1999

Cut to Size

Adapted record, carton, 2001

Toy Story 3

Plastic toys, pencil, gravel, 2005

A number of shafts are sunk into the floor of a room. These are of a depth identical in measurement to the height of the room accommodating various pieces of furniture, for example: settee, armchairs, coffee table, television set, standard lamp. The floor and shafts are carpeted and power is supplied where necessary enabling any electrical items to be turned on.

Floor Level
2007

In a long narrow gallery install
a wind machine at the far end.

Wind Tunnel

2007

Touch

Felt pen, toilet roll, 2006

Repaired Sculpture

Adapted bicycle inner-tube, 2007

Foreign Body

Feather, balloon, 2007

Shuffle

Stockpot, boiling water, playing cards, 2007

A radio is placed inside a wooden box then wrapped in polythene and taped, to make it waterproof. The radio, tuned to BBC Radio One, is switched on at full volume but unplugged. The box is set in a block of concrete from which the electric cable extends allowing the radio to be plugged in.

Set in Concrete
2007

Mud photograph, 1977

If you have encountered Les Coleman's work it is less likely to have been in an art gallery than in the form of a slim book of aphorisms, a pamphlet of drawings, or even just a postcard. These relatively ephemeral and inexpensive items of printed matter have always been an efficient vehicle for Coleman's art, but they are not all he does. Over a forty year period, he has also made unique sculptural objects for exhibitions, as well as installations and site-specific environmental interventions, although most of them do not conform neatly to label writers' taxonomies.

During the early 1970s, in common with other artists in London whose 'experimental' work was difficult to categorise and sell, Coleman found it hard to find places to exhibit. Like others, he relied upon the interest of a small number of independent galleries, that were off-centre, against the grain, and often with limited space. He developed a genre of small-scale, sometimes pocket-size, art objects, partly for this reason, but also due to his domestic circumstances. He calls this 'the aesthetics affected by economics'. But the scale of these works possessed its own appeal for him, being portable and equivalent to a book or a poem, and free from any overweening artistic ambition.

In the tradition of Duchamp's 'readymades', Coleman uses ordinary utilitarian things in the everyday world, and in the parallel tradition of Man Ray's 'treated' found objects and Cage's 'prepared' piano, modifies them in simple ways to render them absurdly unusable. *Cubist Paintbrush*, 1970, for example, is a real paintbrush that has been cut and reassembled to fit its

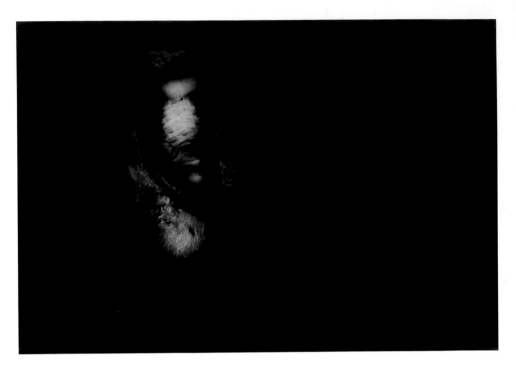

Torchlight photograph, 1978

title but uncertain of its function. In a more recent work *Cut to Size*, 2001, a vinyl LP has been cut to a rectangle to fit snugly into a cardboard box.

The title given to the modified object is an intrinsic part of the work. The reflex action on the part of the viewer to glance from the work of art in an exhibition to its label here satisfyingly completes a cognitive circuit. A hammer with the point of a nail irremovably driven into its head, is called *Revenge*, 1971. A lone table tennis bat that cannot be used to propel the ball that is already embedded in it is called *Game for One*, 1971. For most of their existence, table tennis bats live, immobile, in the darkness of lumber rooms. Do they only become bats when they are taken out and used? Can a lone table tennis bat justify its existence, or does it require possession of an identical partner, a ball, a table, a net, and two players to achieve its performative identity? A later piece *Ping-Pong*, 1996, proposes the installation of a table tennis table in an empty room, without bats, ball or players, only the recorded sound of a game in progress.

All sorts of philosophical trains of thought such as these can be set in motion by these familiar artefacts rendered unfamiliar. Their inferences can be visually understood almost instantly, but are laborious and wordy to describe. So much so, that one almost doesn't want to write about these works. Like good jokes, to explain them serves to make them pedestrian. There is something about the spare, almost puritan, absurdity of these objects that evokes the well known Zen koan about 'the sound of one hand clapping'.

Hand photograph, 1972

While Coleman was a student at Leeds College of Art in the mid-1960s, John Cage's philosophical stance on Zen Buddhism was an influence on him, as it was for many artists and art students at that time. At Leeds, his teachers included Patrick Hughes, Anthony Earnshaw, and the Fluxus artist Robin Page. There he attended lectures by Richard Hamilton on Duchamp, Ron Hunt on Picabia, and Suzi Gablik on Magritte. He saw live performances by Yoko Ono, Bruce Lacey, and Cornelius Cardew. His student thesis was on the dramatist N.F. Simpson, a prime protagonist of a British strain of The Theatre of the Absurd. He became familiar with the writing of Raymond Roussel, Alfred Jarry and Eugène Ionesco, as well as the blurred border between art and life explored by the Fluxus group and the Happenings artists of America and Europe.

Attributes such as blankness, nothingness, emptiness, transparency, and colourlessness, are important elements in quite a number of works. The assemblage *Regatta*, 1991, incorporates a filing cabinet the drawers of which are labelled 'Nothing' with the exception of the only open drawer which is filled with water, on which float a series of paper boats folded from computer paper. Some of the works use unstable or ephemeral materials such as air, water and fresh fruit. *Foreign Body*, 2007, comprises an inflated white balloon containing a feather. The text *Steam*, 1988, proposes a gallery full of buckets of water, the contents of which are to be boiled away during the course of the exhibition, filling the gallery with steam. Other works feature things that are broken, disintegrated or melted, or that have been

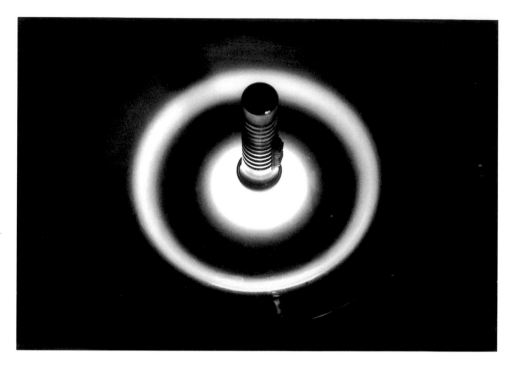

Night Time torch, plate, 1980

made useless. *Set in Concrete*, 2007, proposes silencing a working radio set by encasing it in concrete.

However insubstantial, the materials used in these works are devoid of mystical connotations. They are banal and completely 'obvious'. A series of works feature prosaic empty jam jars. But although Coleman's aim is to achieve clarity and avoid mystification, these works do not reveal themselves in their entirety, as you might initially suppose. Reviewing them uncovers extra significances. Coleman enjoys embracing the incipient poetic or metaphorical aspect accorded to an assemblage of otherwise mundane elements by its title. *Haven*, 1991, is a goldfish bowl full of oil in which sits a collection of ball bearings.

The extreme reduction of means in many of these works may seem to align them with minimalist and conceptualist works. A group of wall-hung works made in the mid-1970s, comprising very simple arrangements of objects such as nails, chalks, and rubber bands held in tension, employ the understatement and economy of means of the minimalist aesthetic. The stylistic trademarks of conceptual art, in its unalloyed, strictly applied mode, are equally present in Coleman's work: plain documentary photography of everyday objects or situations, non-literary textual content, the deployment of a rigidly systematic, process-led praxis, but almost as a commentary upon such devices, at a distance from the strict ethos that lay behind them. The labels stuck to the apples in *Possession*, 1980, mimic the stylistic tropes of conceptual art, while the photographs of the works *Air and Water*, 1975, and *Chalks*, 1975,

Display plates, wire display stands, 1987

have very much the 'look' of the inscrutably objective photographs that were printed on exhibition invitation cards from galleries specialising in conceptual art, and which often looked like something out of a physics textbook.

The laws of physics do insinuate themselves, in fact, into some of these works. A wheel of test tubes makes manifest *The Effect of Gravity on Water*, 1995, a burning candle is slowly *Losing Weight*, 1996, as it sits on a set of scales, and ink has leaked from a felt tip pen into a toilet roll that it has been allowed to *Touch*, 2006.

Familiar figures of speech are rendered absurd by being taken literally. *Dust Trap*, 1973, is just what it says. It has no other purpose. It is a piece of cartridge paper crumpled up into a palm-sized shape, and covered entirely in household paint of a deep red hue. It has hardened into an exquisite little *objet d'art*, like the head of an exotic ornamental cabbage, or one of those convoluted natural stones revered by Taoists. Part ornament, part sculpture, its reason for existence being to attract dust, sitting on a mantelpiece for thirty years before disintegrating.

Packaging of anything, an artist's *oeuvre*, a political ideology, is a recurrent theme in Coleman's work, either overtly or as a sub-text. Some of these small-scale art objects are about art, and the 'packaging' of art. They reflect upon the nature of contemporary art and particularly the celebrity status of artists and their stylistic trademarks, which come to lead lives of their own as the artist's 'brand'. There is the way, for example, that the professional

Spent can of shaving foam, 1985

tools of a famous artist (such as Turner's palette in the Tate Gallery) are fetishised and exhibited as holy relics in public museums. So the surface of *Pollock's Palette*, 1971, replicates the appearance of one of Jackson Pollock's drip paintings, in the way that a cartoon by Maurice Henri shows Picasso painting the portrait of a model whose actual physiognomy is as fractured as the artist's Cubist style.

The uniqueness of the work does not concern him. Indeed much of his work as an artist is concerned actively to erode the entrenched partnership between visual art and exclusivity. Some of the works from common bought objects have been made more than once. Nevertheless, some objects, rather perversely, are carefully crafted facsimiles of everyday objects, a strategy that he still enjoys employing. For *Pollock's Palette*, for example, he could have purchased a 'readymade' palette from an artists' supplies shop, but instead chose to make one.

Coleman also refers in his works to the general habits, etiquette and politics of art galleries: such things as the private view, the gallery comments book, the customary arrangement of valuable exhibits on plinths and their propensity to elevate even something valueless to the realm of art. In *Anyone for Sculpture?*, 1988, a delapidated and defunct tennis ball is enshrined on a cased plinth surrounded by a rope barrier. *Accident*, 1991, comprises an empty plinth with the remains of a broken china ornament on the floor alongside.

The printed matter that unfailingly accompanies exhibitions of contemporary art, engineering

Magnified Weight weight, magnifying glass, 1992

its subsequent place in the art historical canon. Several of the works incorporate exhibition catalogues, postcards of modern art, or other artists' statements. *Dividing Line*, 1983, a fault line across the gallery floor defined by truncated postcards of 20th century art, is reminiscent of one of the kind of site-specific floor installations that characterised the influential conceptual art show 'When Attitudes Become Form' in 1969.

Sometimes the art reference in the work is obvious and direct. *1lb of Sugar*, 1975, is such an amount of sugar cubes laid out as a formal rectangle: an echo of Carl Andre's minimally formal 'Equivalent VIII', aka the 'Tate bricks', purchased by the Tate Gallery (and hence the sugar reference to Tate & Lyle) in 1972. Not so direct are the possible references in a number of his works involving jam jars and drinking glasses to another work owned by the Tate, Michael Craig Martin's 'An Oak Tree', 1973, which is the title accorded by the artist to an artistically transubstantiated glass of water on a shelf.

Sometimes several objects are placed together within a space, in effect creating a small installation. One such work is *England v. Italy*, 1981. In a darkened gallery, an English domestic electric fire and a small Italian electric fan are positioned facing each other, one emitting heat and the other blowing cool air. Both appliances are wired together into a single electric plug, thus using the power to opposing effect. Exploiting the propensity of inanimate objects to suggest human characteristics, this work can be construed as performance art for objects, or small-scale visual theatre.

£150 £50 notes, glass, 1983

Although Coleman could never be mistaken for a performance artist, much of his work elicits a low-level performative response from the viewer, if only in their attempt to prise apart the pages of his publication *Glue*, 2002, or having to turn over a double-sided postcard to read the mirrored text on both sides. A certain kind of interactivity, not the spurious sort currently prevalent in our public art galleries and museums, is also set in motion by some of the object-based work, countering the passivity that is part of viewing a traditional exhibit in an art gallery. In *The Little Green Aeroplane Joins In*, 1983, a live TV set relays whatever is being broadcast with the mischievous added presence of a catapulted plastic toy plane stuck by its suction cap to the screen.

Most of these objects are table-top size. But Coleman is just as interested in the table itself. Tables, chairs, furniture, and doors all appear in his works, looking like they might have come from one of the random assemblages of the Fluxus artist George Brecht. In some of his exhibitions, the actual fabric of the art gallery, and its fittings, have been re-built or interfered with. *Entrance*, 1995, introduces an actual door and its frame set disconcertingly at an angle into the middle of the white gallery wall, achieving a sort of anti-*trompe l'oeil* effect. In *360°*, 1984, a copy of a modern atlas in its shiny dust wrapper seems to have become immovably lodged between the wall and the gallery floor, inducing a feeling of constriction contrary to the unlimited horizons contained within such a volume.

When the opportunity has presented itself, Coleman has made works for one occasion only,

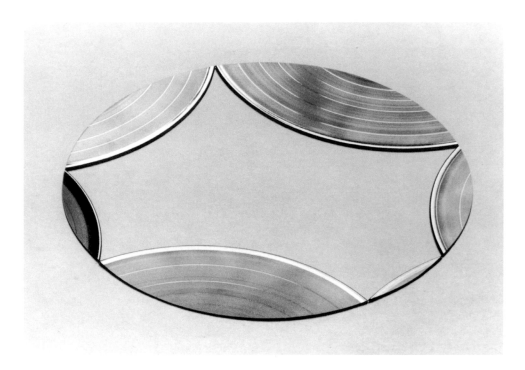

33rpm cut record, 1983

and specially for one place. These days they would be known as 'site-specific installations', or in certain cases 'interventions' in an interior or exterior public space. An example of the latter was *12 Fournier Street, London E1*, 1981, a saloon car parked outside the house of the artists Gilbert and George in Spitalfields. On the car windscreen, the names of the two artists are emblazoned, a work made for 'The Motor Show'. Other sites outside an art context for which he has made special art works have ranged from a flag bearing a barcode taken from a Union Jack postcard and titled *National Pride*, 1994, to a large pile of books appearing to float in mid-air in the window of a public library, *Mind Over Matter*, 1994.

Some of Coleman's gallery and site-specific installations have been surprisingly complicated, given the striking simplicity of his object works. *Survival Circle*, 1984, involved a schematic ground plan, and a related arrangement of small metal puzzles, live snails and lettuce. *Hammersmith Broadway*, 1993, was devised for the public area of a community arts centre using eight slide projectors and recorded sounds. The layout of this intervention incorporated the shadows cast by visitors to the gallery as they obstructed the images thrown by the projectors. Coleman has said that he sees the work as reflecting the 'organised chaos' of its source.

Patrick Hughes's epigram about Les Coleman cannot be bettered: "Les is more". The most drastically reduced of his works are those that do not actually exist. That is, they have not yet been made. They exist only as short descriptive texts, as spare and concise as his

Mr. Hirst is Exceedingly Rich Swiss roll cake, 2006

arrangements of three-dimensional objects. These texts can be construed as works in themselves, and in this respect they can be aligned with the text-works written by conceptual artists, and the short text-scores written during the 1960s by composers such as Karlheinz Stockhausen and LaMonte Young.

Some of Coleman's texts describe works that could be made, some would be difficult but not impossible to make, and a few are impossible to make. The text piece called *Unrealisable Sculpture*, 1995, is laid out typographically like the texts that accompany the photographic works of Richard Long or Hamish Fulton. Its title, and its specifications for an absurd Himalayan Range of cutlery bring to mind the words of the absurdist columnist Beachcomber: "Sixty horses wedged in a chimney. The story to fit this headline has not turned up yet".

What saves Coleman from being a po-faced conceptualist on the one hand, or a twee assemblage artist on the other, is the inclusion in his work of healthy doses of bathos, a word not much discussed or analysed these days in relation to visual art.

Where Joseph Beuys has fat and felt, Coleman has lard and tiddlywinks. As Kounellis brought live horses into the art gallery, Coleman has exhibited live snails and dead flies. He has applied the formal process inherent in a sculpture by Damien Hirst to a Swiss roll.

The influences of Duchamp and Cage upon Coleman's work have met with an equal and not entirely opposite force from things like British post-war radio comedy, comics and cartooning. For Coleman, the extravagant graphic imaginations of Roland Topor, Siné or Robert Crumb,

Launch of *Kinds of Clouds*, 1981

and the *double entendres* of Donald McGill and the drawings of Saul Steinberg are as serious and important as anything in the mainstream canon of 20th century fine art. Coleman has also known and revered such artists as Anthony Earnshaw, the Belgian Surrealist Marcel Mariën, the reclusive Fluxus artist George Brecht – people who never were, and never would be accepted into the fold of the career *biennalisti*.

As a member of the art world, Coleman 'joins in'. But only up to a point. Coleman hovers between targeted critical attack and quizzical disengagement, like the little green aeroplane in his work of the same name.

Les Coleman was born in Kirk Ella, Yorkshire in 1945 and attended Hull, Leeds and Goldsmiths Colleges of Art variously between 1962 and 1984. He has lived in London since 1967.

Selected Exhibitions: 1976—*Leedz 3 Varieties*, (with Jonet Harley-Peters and Tim Mitchell), Battersea Arts Centre, London. 1978—*February*, Coracle Press, London. 1980—*A New Order*, Front Room, London; *Made in King Kong*, (with Tony Blundell and Anthony Earnshaw), Greenwich Theatre Gallery, London. 1981—*Room Temperature*, Southampton Art Gallery, Southampton; *England v Italy*, Coracle Press, London. 1983—*Artist of the Day*, Angela Flowers Gallery, London. 1988—*Headache*, Battersea Arts Centre, London; *Les Coleman and Patrick Hughes*, Dean Clough Contemporary Art Gallery, Halifax. 1990—*In the Air*, Arndale Shopping Centre, Wandsworth and Battersea Arts Centre, London; *Good Boy*, 109 Charing Cross Road, London; *Pictureplay*, Chelsea Arts Club, London. 1991—*Collected Works*, Fouts & Fowler Gallery, London. 1993—*Hammersmith Broadway*, Central Space, London; *A Dog Called Trigger and Other Drawings*, Angela Flowers Gallery, London; *Words & Pictures*, Bluecoat Gallery, Liverpool. 1994—*Mind Over Matter*, Hammersmith Area Library, London. 1995—*Double Vision*, (with Peter Ellis), Crossley Gallery, Halifax; *Made to Measure*, Hardware Gallery, London. 1996—*Meet the Art Students*, 109 Charing Cross Road, London; *Daft as Two Brushes*, (with Peter Ellis), Gallerie du Cirque Divers, Liège. 1997—*The Almost Complete Meet the Art Students*, Jago, London. 2002—*Les Coleman In Print 1967–2002*, bookartbookshop, London. 2003—*Drawings and Prints*, Boekie Woekie, Amsterdam. 2004—*Meet the Art Students, A Brief History*, Templeman Library, University of Kent, Canterbury; *Knives, Forks and Spoons*, (with Charlie Holmes), bookartbookshop, London; *Books, Pamphlets and Printed Ephemera*, School of Art Library, UWE, Bristol. 2005—*Night Light*, 60 Peckham Road, London; *Pinboard Gallery*, bookartbookshop, London. 2006—*Les Coleman's Grand Sale*, Studio Show, London.

Selected Publications: 1973—*The Jewish Banana*, Number Nineteen, London. 1981—*Kinds of Clouds*, Coracle Press, London. 1982—*With My Right Hand*, White Lies Publications, London. 1989—*180 Grammes*, In House Publishing, London and Newcastle. 1990—*In the Air*, Battersea Arts Centre, London. 1991—*Yin and Yang*, (with Patrick Hughes), Copy Book, London. 1992—*Unthoughts*, Ink Sculptors, London. 1993—*Unthinking*, Littlewood Arc, Todmorden. 1994—*Impénsees*, Hourglass, Paris; *Bookmark*, (with Charlie Holmes), In House Publishing, London and Newcastle. 1995—*Colemania*, Hardware Gallery, London. 1996—*Black Ink*, In House Publishing, London and Newcastle. 1997—*Meet the Art Students*, Arc Publications, Todmorden; *Dislocation*, (with Tony Blundell, Anthony Earnshaw and Chris Vine), Copy Book, London; *Meet the Art Students* (concertina), Hayvend, London; *Forks*, (with Charlie Holmes), In House Publishing, London and Newcastle. 2002—*Scrap Book*, (with John Dilnot), self-published; *Little Critic 16*, Coracle, Ballybeg, Ireland; *Meet the Art Students: Now in Glorious Crayon*, In House Publishing, London and Oxford; *The Professors*, In House Publishing, London and Oxford; *Unthunk*, Errata, Stockholm. 2004—*Je suis trop vieux pour mourir jeune*, Station Underground d'Emerveillement Littéraire, Ligny-lez-Aire, France. 2005—*Flux Paper Events Revisited*, self-published; *Imperfect Sense*, In House Publishing, London and Oxford. 2006—*In Brief: Volume I and Volume II*, In House Publishing, London and Oxford. 2007—*Thunks*, Redfoxpress, Dugort, Ireland. 2008—*The Book of The Show*, In House Publishing, London and Oxford; *c for Brecht* (editor) Redfoxpress, Dugort, Ireland. 2009—*Afterthunks*, Boekie Woekie, Amsterdam.

Thanks to The Elephant Trust and Sarah Whitfield; and to Colin Sackett, David Briers, Nancy Fouts, Patrick Hughes, John Bevis and Simon Cutts for their generous contributions and advice given.

Photo credits: Martin Cook p.80; John Dilnot p.50, 57; Liz Ford p.41–43; Nancy Fouts p.18, 66, 71–74, 85, 87; Jonet Harley-Peters p.12–13, 81; Charlie Holmes p.15, 21, 29, 37, 41, 44–45, 51–53, 56, 82–84, 86; Nathan Kelly p.60–63; Shaun McCracken p.39–40; George Ong p.68–69; Tanya Peixoto p.88; Colin Sackett p.9, cover; Brian Lane p.89.